Write To Grow

Build Your Business, Get More Clients, Make More Money

By Colleen Walsh Fong

Written in loving memory of

My first business writing coach,

My Dad.

He taught me everything I needed to know

To make my business grow.

And he did it all his way.

Table of Contents

Chapter 1

Why You Have to Write to Get Business

When a tree falls in the forest it *does* make a sound. But if no one hears it, the impact is lost. When business owners write content to attract and retain clients it exists. But if it isn't read it doesn't get the intended results.

Writing to reach clients remains one of the best ways to grow your business. According to 2014 information published by ignitespot.com almost 61% of consumers have made a purchase based on a blog post. This may be because reading blogs and social platforms makes up 23% of the time people spend on the Internet. Seventy seven percent of Internet users read blogs and a whopping 81% of US consumers trust advice and information from blogs. *Most amazingly, 70% of consumers learn about a company through articles rather than ads.*[1]

Television and radio sound bites can drive business. And sound bites combined with more detailed and persuasive written information about a product or service wields power. The more of it you can get in front of people, the better. So before you even ask I will tell you. Yes! You *do* need continual, written content to grow your business.

We've all heard the old adage, "absence makes the heart grow fonder." It may be true where romance is concerned. But it definitely does not apply to growing your business. "Out of sight, out of mind," is more apt for that situation.

Getting and keeping clients requires regular, ongoing communication.

Why?

Let me count the reasons.

---

1   ignitespot http://blog.ignitespot.com

Reason #1–People Are on Option Overload

It's easy to get lost in the blizzard of options blanketing the average person each day. My email inbox is stuffed with new information about all kinds of things every morning. I see more interesting stuff when I check in on my daily news sources. And even more things grab my eyes as I scroll through Facebook posts.

I can't even buy a cup of coffee without having to answer two or three questions to clarify my order. The other day a new item appeared on the menu board at my local java shop–Flat White. The description made it sound stronger than my usual short latte, which would have caused me to change my go-to order. The barista couldn't explain the difference, though, and I needed my caffeine. Also, the line behind me had filled with toe-tappers, impatient to get their coffee and go. So I stuck with what I knew would meet my needs. But I was intrigued enough that if I'd had a more knowledgeable server or a shorter queue behind me I may have abandoned my devotion to short lattes and jumped ship with the newest java fad.

Your clients and potential clients are being similarly bombarded with new options to what you do. It's important to remind them often that you're there for them so a newcomer to your business niche doesn't lure them away.

Will you drive clients away if you keep putting your brand in front of them?

No.

It may be hard to believe that repeated contact won't make you seem like a gnat under the sweat-soaked sunglasses of a Biloxi, Mississippi resident in July. But the truth is that even if it does, you'll still end up attracting and retaining more customers—especially if you share useful information. This is because most people can only come up with one or two names when they think about specialists. And the names they come up with most often are those they hear or see most frequently.

We unconsciously equate quantity with quality. So the name we hear the most often gets translated into the brand we believe is the best. This phenomenon was noticed as long ago as 1885 when Thomas Smith, an early expert on advertising, observed that people bought a product or service after the 20th time they heard its name.

When I was a residential realtor another local realtor plastered her name and face on every surface she could find. On her car. On her signs. Even on the walls of the local recreational sports facilities. She had a column in a local print magazine and later on an online hyper-local news source. Her listings yielded the lowest sale price of local realtors year after year. I had the documentation to prove it. But if you asked people to name the best realtor in the area, her name crossed lips most often. Since her face, her name, and her helpful columns were everywhere, people equated that quantity with quality, often at significant financial loss to themselves. I had to hand it to her. She cornered the market by staying in front of the client pool.

One of the most successful ad campaigns of the 20th century featured finicky grocer, Mr. Whipple, chiding customers for squeezing the Charmin. For years the commercials played relentlessly on TV, much to my chagrin. I found them exceedingly annoying. But guess which brand I've stocked in my home for decades? Charmin. Go figure. The commercials rankle, but the brand is stuck in my brain.

Does the following chant, "Hudson 3, 2, 7-hundred," mean anything to you? If you lived in Metro Chicago in the 1970's I bet it rings a bell. I heard it scads of times on WGN when growing up. I may not always remember what I walked into a room to fetch, but the telephone number to an upholstery cleaning service I heard repeatedly more than thirty years ago hiccups up out of nowhere when the subject of upholstery comes up. And because I've written branding content for home décor publications and interior design firms that topic has come up often.

Suffice it to say that other members of your business niche will become the brand brains default to if you don't seize that opportunity.

Reason #2–Regular Communication Generates Sales

Communication output, like blogs, newsletters, and press releases gives you an easy way to let your customers know about new products, services, promotions, or pricing changes. Feeding your platforms with useful information helps you to grow your reader base. And interactive ones, like blogs and websites give your readers a way to give you feedback about how you're doing. That information can improve your business by leading you to adopt new approaches or offer new products and services.

Interactive platforms, like blogs, also give you the chance to ask your base for referrals. And they help you grow your readership when you make your communications shareable through email and various social media sites.

Reason #3–Communicating Helps Maintain Healthy Relationships

Throughout most of the 20th century customers had real, personal, daily interactions with the people they bought things from. They knew their butchers, grocers, dry cleaners, bankers, and ser-vice-station attendants on a personal level. They knew these people by their names and chances are they knew their families, too.

I liked Ray, the dry cleaner who picked up my dad's worn dress shirts and dropped off the cleaned and pressed ones each week. I remember him especially well because Wednesdays, when he stopped at our house, were "cardboard days." That meant whichever kid happened to be around could nab the cardboard my dad's fresh shirts were wrapped around and use them for art projects. And Ray always brought a couple of extra cardboard sheets up to the door for us because he knew we kids liked them.

My mom telephoned her grocery order to Sonny who lived down the street and ran the local grocery. He made weekly deliveries. If something was missing from the delivered boxes my mom just sent one of us kids down the street to let him know. He'd usually reward the messenger with a trinket, like a pencil or an eight-pack of crayons. Those personal relationships meant something. They made it easy for my parents to get what they needed and to have special needs taken care of.

But they also helped the business owners to build brand loyalty. It's easy to anticipate clients' needs when you know them well. And you can throw in a little something extra to keep customers happy when you know what they like. Which makes it even harder for them to cut off your professional relationship.

Have you ever had to tell someone you know personally that you're not going to buy from him? When you have a relationship with your service provider it's almost as hard to buy from someone else as it is to say "No" to the little girl next door who's selling Girl Scout cookies.

Reason #4–Everyone Is On The Internet

I knew the electronic age had arrived when my 70-something uncle started emailing me with his jokes in the 1990's. And my sister confirmed it when she told me a few years back that her 80-year old father-in-law preferred tweeting to texting because it reached more friends faster. A recent study by the Pew Research Center confirmed my assumptions. It found that almost 60% of

Americans aged 65 or older use the Internet. Forty-seven percent have high-speed connection in their homes and 77% use cell phones.[2]

This tells us that the face-to-face, local relationships between business owners and their customers can be replaced by Internet relationships with people of all ages. The downside of this scenario is dealing with the Internet's anonymity.

The upside is that the Internet has opened up a whole world of customers to businesses, and of vendor options to buyers. As brick and mortar stores close down because they can't compete with the likes of Amazon and other high-volume online sellers, both buyers and sellers stand to lose or to gain depending upon whether they use the Internet to their advantages or disadvantages.

Say what?

You have a choice. You can play the current state of affairs to your advantage as a business owner by finding ways to develop online relationships with your client pool. Or you can leave that to your competition. Smart business owners find ways

---

2   http://www.pewinternet.org/2014/04/03/older-adults-and-technology-use/

to be welcomed into their customers' computers, phones, and tablets in the same way that Jimmy Fallon and Jimmy Kimmel are welcomed into their homes each night.

People have a hard time saying goodbye to characters they've come to know and love. That's why trilogies have become such a coveted commodity. Stephanie Meyers' "Twilight" series, Ken Follett's "Century" trilogy, and Suzanne Collins' "Hunger Games" trilogy were top sellers. Think about your favorite TV show. Do the characters feel like friends, even though you've never met? Do you look forward to seeing them each day or each week? Do you miss them when the season ends? If so you are in a virtual relationship.

Smart business owners use the Internet to develop the same kinds of relationships with clients they will never meet. And this book will teach *you* how to do that too.

Chapter 2

Where to Communicate

Everyone needs a website. Period.

Your website is your electronic home. It's where you hang your metaphorical hat. You decorate it to reflect your personality and to show off all your cool stuff. It should tell visitors:

1. Who You Are
2. What You Do
3. Where You Do It
4. How It Helps Them
5. How They Can Get It

It should reflect your corporate personality.

It should offer helpful information to visitors—refreshments, so to speak. Here are some of the things you can serve.

Free Download

White papers make good free downloads. They are documents that outline a problem or challenge and then explain how the product or service you offer solves that problem. Depending upon what that is they can contain charts and citations to support your conclusions, or they can be more conversational.

White papers work best when they are subtle sales tools that give clients useful information about how to go about something, but suggest that using your product or service will accomplish their objectives more easily, more professionally, or in a more cost-effective way.

These documents are usually stored in a PDF format on your website with a click-through option. Visitors who wish to download the free information click on the link or icon provided.

Their contact information is collected for your future marketing campaigns. They receive your free information. You get their contact information and the opportunity to pitch your product or service to them often without their realizing you are marketing.

Blog Posts

I use blogs every day. I have one on each of my websites and I blog on several "open access" sites, too.

Blog posts are short articles. They can be opinion pieces, contain factual information, or make a point with an amusing anecdote. Readers can comment on blog posts, so this tool gives you a way to have a virtual conversation with your readers. They should contain useful and attention-grabbing information and it should be shareable through social media. Blogs are a great way to develop a virtual relationship with existing and potential customers.

Articles

Articles can be longer than blog posts, and are usually a little more formal. They can reside on a special page of your site and be downloadable like white papers. And you can submit them to various media outlets such as trade journals, your local newspapers, print and online magazines, and regional and national publications, too. Articles are a one-way communication stream through which you give information or opinion.

Coupons

If you sell a product or service you may want to host downloadable coupons on your site. If you have an e-commerce site from which visitors can buy products or services via a shopping cart you may want to consider using a coupon code that can be plugged in during the checkout process.

Coupons can be advertised in other places, such as ads on social media sites, like Facebook, which has a built-in ad function. Ads can be placed on online news-sources, and other privately owned websites that enable ad functions. Google

AdSense is probably the best known, but many other sources, such as Intellilinks, Clicksor, and ProGrids, exist, too.

Special Offers

Service-based businesses can offer promotions on their services or packages for limited time periods. Placing the offer on your site may be enough to generate a buzz if you have a good readership and a solid Twitter or Facebook following to announce it through.

Attract even more potential buyers by announcing coupons and special offers in blog posts.

Videos and Slide Shows

Videos and slide shows are great ways to show off your product or service. Brief how-to videos can attract visitors to sites. Are you a Realtor? Videos on home-maintenance or room staging are useful to visitors, and great hooks for bringing new eyes to your site. Produce your own and share them on your YouTube channel with links back to your site. Host them on your site, too. Or simply embed videos produced by others into your blog posts.

Slick slide shows are another visual medium that can give valuable information to visitors. When hosted on other platforms they can direct viewers to your site.

The goal of all these virtual toys is to get people to your site and keep them there so they look at your product or service offerings. And to keep them coming back, sharing your information, and recommending it to friends.

Website Format

Make sure your site is easy to navigate. People frustrate easily. They won't hang around if they can't find what they're looking for, or anything that interests them.

So give them quality content, and keep your format simple and clearly labeled.

Put yourself in the buyers' shoes. What would you need to see or to know to buy your product or service? Make sure that information is on your site.

Be prolific yet brief. This sounds like a contradiction but it isn't. It just means you need to turn the information tap on to a drizzle. Produce new content regularly to give visitors a reason to go to your site. And make sure it's brief so you don't lose their interest.

Make sure your site is SEO friendly. That means content can be optimized so the search engines can find it easily.

Website Sources

If you have an existing website tweak it to conform to the advice listed above.

If you don't have a website, and you're not sure where to get one, there are many free website sources. I've used Weebly, WordPress, and Blogger. Of those three I like WordPress best. It's user-friendly and is good for SEO.

Chapter 3

Where to Get Writing Ideas

Whether you already have a website, blog, or newsletter; or you are in the process of developing one or all of them, you need good content to get the results required to make your business successful. Where do you get ideas for your content?

I find everything organic is best. Organic foods are popular because they're produced without harmful chemicals and additives. They contain few artificial ingredients. Organic ideas are similarly free from artificial and stilted concepts, scenarios, and language. So they ring true with readers and resonate with more people.

Let your content ideas come to you organically from your daily experiences and observations. And feel free to weave in some anecdotes from your past too. Just keep it real. Readers can smell a contrivance a mile away.

Let's take the TV sitcom for example. Even from the get-go this format had credibility problems. I'm stretching back into the past a pretty long way, but I don't know anyone who had a "Leave It To Beaver" family. My mom definitely didn't vacuum the house wearing a string of pearls. Or a "Brady Bunch" family. My stay-at-home mom didn't have a live-in maid like Alice.

Things got a little more real in the 1980's with "Growing Pains" and "Family Ties" because of the snarky sibling commentary and working moms who cleaned their own homes. But I never knew a kid with the kind of corporate savvy of Alex P. Keaton, or a dad like Jason Seaver who seemed to always be around. When did he meet with his patients? And the Olson twins' portrayal of precocious Michelle, saying, "You've got it, dude," and "How rude!" may have been good for laughs but was not realistic.

I love Modern Family, too, but how many times can Dee-Dee attack Gloria and get invited back to a family event? If you prefer dramatic examples to sit-com ones, how many miracle surgeries can the good doctors of Grey's Anatomy perform in one season? What are the odds of that many unusual cases landing in one hospital and being cured by on-the-spot, ingenious, newly developed techniques in one 6-month run?

Even the current trend of reality TV doesn't feel real. I was a competition dance mom and none of my fellow moms or me cursed each other out. Nor do I see any ZZ Top-type characters selling moonshine when I go up into the North Georgia and Smokey Mountains.

And forgive me, but I choked on my drink at a local open-mic night when I heard a 17-year old country-music wannabe sing his new composition about drinking whiskey while riding the freight trains. Besides being grossly under-age, he'd rolled up in a pretty nice ride. I wanted to ask him, "Dude, what freight trains? Where would you even find one to hop these days?" I quickly tuned him out. Characters and entertainers can only hold interest as long as people feel a genuine connection with them. To make a genuine connection, you have to *be* genuine.

Once you get busted for insincerity it's hard to come back. Look at what happened to Geraldo Rivera as a result of his Iraq War whopper, and more recently to Brian Williams for his Hurricane Katrina fib.

Sticking to the truth and to what you know is the best way to be taken seriously. How can you do that? By using your genuine, every day observations and experiences as the basis for producing content.

Keep Your Eyes and Ears Open

It's always fun to people watch. When you are out and about pay attention to the people around you. Watch what they are saying and doing. Notice what they're wearing. When you see things that are out of the ordinary make note of them. What is your gut reaction to what you saw or heard? What did it make you think about? Does it relate in any way to what you do for a living? Or to what your customers' needs might be?

I watched four women scroll through and tap away at the screens of their individual phones while lunching together. They could have been eating alone at a lunch counter for all the interacting they did. I turned that observation into a blog post about the many electronic interruptions we get throughout the day and how attending to them hurts our relationships. Then I tweaked it for a client who provides sales coaching, and included three tips for holding potential clients' attention to develop strong relationships. It worked because it came from a real event that almost everyone has seen or done. Readers could relate to it.

Keep a Log

Do ideas jump into your head when you're walking the dog or driving home from work? Use the voice memo function on your hands-free phone to make a note about them so you don't forget them. Later, before you go to bed or before you start your day each morning play the memos back and jot down some notes to elaborate on how you can use them.

Keeping a daily log or diary of the important events of your day can give you a rich source of writing ideas, too. I like to write down my stream-of-consciousness thoughts each morning. It's a practice I started some years ago when doing *The Artist's Way* program developed by Julia Cameron. A writer friend recommended it to me as a way to free-up writer's block. The program calls for starting your day by writing three pages of whatever comes into your mind. There are many reasons why this program works, and it has other applications, too. For more information about it I recommend purchasing Cameron's book.

I've continued stream of consciousness writing each morning, but these days it usually amounts to a page or less. The exercise gets my pen going and my mind into the writing zone. It clears out my thought cache, too. Then I read what I wrote and highlight things I want to think or write more about, and that helps me to create my daily to-do list. A bounty of topic ideas has come to me this way.

One morning I found myself dwelling on a comment a young friend had made to me about *needing* a new car. This person owned an old but working vehicle, was laden with debt, and under-employed. So I couldn't help focusing on her notion of what constituted a necessity. It prompted an article about the difference between need-to-have and nice-to-have, and how important knowing the difference can be to financial success. I wrote it for a client who does financial planning. I later tweaked that message to fit a number of situations and audiences including business owners, managers, parents, and interior designers. I freed my mind of something that bothered me and hit pay dirt in the idea-generation department.

Relate Your Observations to Your Clients' Needs

Once you've recorded your observations and made your notes, think about how those things might relate to your clients' needs. Are you in the automobile insurance business? What dangerous practices have you seen on the road lately? Has someone pulled out of a parking spot without looking? Did a client let his oil level get too low and ruin his car when the engine seized up? Did you walk past a sap-covered car parked under a tree? Turn your observations into short blog posts covering tips for keeping cars damage free.

Spin It

Once you get a good idea, think about how else you can use it. See if you can spin it into other blog or article topics. Then try to make it fit different audiences. That way you get the most out of your brainchildren. I call this Rumplestiltspinning because, like the fairy tale character, Rumplestiltskin, it gives you a way to spin something ordinary into gold.

I take a single idea and set the timer on my phone for two minutes. I write as many twists on that idea as I can while the timer runs. I write quickly and feel good when I get 10 ideas down on paper during the two-minute time limit.

I spun the single topic idea, how I react to receiving bad customer service, into ten more:

1. What happens to sales when customers are unable to get help in your store?

2. Will you get return business from customers when you miss your due date?

3. How can you keep clients who have experienced bad customer service?

4. How to train your employees to give good customer service.

5. Why does customer service matter?

6. The impact of customer service on your bottom line.

7. Do you know what your employees are telling your clients?

8. The impact of ignoring a customer.

9. Is your business immune to the side effects of bad customer service?

10. How to test whether your employees have been well-trained.

Give it a try. You'll be surprised how many things you can come up with when you challenge yourself.

Chapter 4

Give Something of Value in Everything You Write

Everybody loves to get free stuff. If you think you're exempt from that truism I bet I can prove you wrong with a few questions.

Have you ever tried a free sample in the grocery store, or when you walked through the food court at the local mall?

Do you use the free movie coupons Redbox sends to you through email?

Do you accept free samples in cosmetic stores?

Do you download free apps to your mobile devices?

Have you ever taken a bar of soap, shampoo, or towel from a hotel? Or picked a hotel for its complimentary breakfast or free coffee? Or enjoyed the chocolates placed upon your pillow?

Do you ever get wined and dined by vendors or sales people?

Do you like company SWAG? Or like to give it to your spouse or kids?

You get the point. Free stuff is fun. It lifts our spirits and makes us feel special. Getting free stuff is like getting an unexpected gift. And when you give it out it can pay off in a big way by attracting new customers or clients and building brand loyalty.

The Bottomless Margarita

Once upon a time there was a little mom and pop Mexican restaurant within walking distance of our home. It served some excellent dishes. The owners catered to families by letting kids roam around the big dining room. On any Friday evening half of the neighborhood would eat there with their kids. A mariachi band entertained the wee ones on weekend nights while parents sipped frozen margaritas. The owners knew our faces, where we liked to sit, and what we liked to drink. And they let us linger for as long as we liked. That restaurant gave us our Friday night entertainment for years.

Then one day another Mexican restaurant opened up just around the corner from our neighborhood hang out. The owner of the new restaurant put buy-one-get-one-free (BOGO) coupons in the weekly mailer. So a bunch of us stood in a long line that Friday night to get a table in the new restaurant. The food was more ordinary and not as tasty as what they served at our usual place. And the room was small so kids couldn't visit around, and four families couldn't sit together at one big table. But the owner came around with an ever-flowing pitcher of frozen margaritas and refilled our glasses for free throughout the entire meal.

I wasn't that impressed with the new spot. Most of our Friday night was spent waiting in line. The free margarita refills were nice, but they were watered down and I would have enjoyed my drinks more if I'd been able to sit with all my friends. My kids missed the mariachi band and being able to run around with their buddies. But the rest of our group loved the great deal and so we continued to frequent the new spot. Soon that owner knew all of our particulars and ratcheted up the return on our investment in his restaurant by honoring expired BOGO coupons. One patron had hers laminated and hung it from her key chain.

Within a year our original hangout was like a ghost town. Even when the new place earned a low health department score, and pictures of the reasons for that score were posted on a hyperlocal news source site, business at the original Mexican restaurant didn't pick up. It eventually closed. People would not give up their bottomless margaritas no matter what.

That's what free stuff can do—attract new customers and keep them.

Giving builds brand loyalty. People will return to a business or locale because they can get something they like for nothing. Many also feel obligated to repay the debt with their business. In the case of the Mexican restaurant, the owner found something he could give away that didn't cost him much—watered down margaritas. And it paid off in a big way.

Create Your Own Concoction

Your challenge is to find your bottomless margarita. Something you can give away that won't cut into your profits and something that relates to what you do. And then give something of value to your readers in every communication so they keep coming back for more.

Does that sound like an overwhelming task? It's easier than you think, because there is a whole world full of information, knowledge, and tips to give.

Start by brainstorming to come up with something that relates to what you do. In my case I make sure every blog post I write has some useful information about some aspect of getting a message across to readers. Sometimes it is as simple as a commonly overlooked grammar rule. Sometimes it's more complex information about changes in search engine formulas. Sometimes I give information about how to do something that will grow readers' businesses. All of those things relate to what I do for a living.

In the food blog used to promote my cookbooks I offer information about food and cooking, and occasionally give away free recipes. Many readers have enjoyed the sample of what my cookbooks offer enough to buy my books and to recommend them to others. I regularly receive "how-to" questions from readers because they think of me when they think of cooking.

Some realtors write weekly or monthly tips about things homeowners should do to care for their homes during that period. For example, my realtor reminded me that late summer is a good time to change furnace filters and have the furnace inspected. Others send newsletters containing local sales information. Still others provide a free moving van to their clients, or yard sale signs bearing the realtor's name. So when local residents see that realtor's logo or face on a moving van or yard sale sign they begin to associate that realtor with actions having to do with buying or selling a home.

I write for a recruiter who gives dress-for-success tips to job candidates and interviewing tips to hiring managers. A local CPA client writes monthly reminders of all the things her small business clients should do that month to get ready for tax filing time.

A local house cleaning business writes about green cleaning tips and ways to save money on home maintenance. When readers use those tips they think about the source of them and begin to associate that business with cleaning services.

Writing useful information about things related to what you do helps to make you a household word or make yourself synonymous with the thing you do. Then, when people think about hiring someone to do the thing you do, they think of you first.

The trick is to give enough to make your information useful to readers and to make them want to come back for more while leaving them with information about how you can do it for them better, faster, or at a lower cost. That takes lots of thought, planning, and practice.

Chapter 5

What to Write

If you haven't written marketing material before it can be hard to know where to start. The good news is there is a whole world full of things to write about. Some were covered in Chapter 3. But there are many more types of things you can write about to attract customers or clients to your business.

Introductory Information

When you're just starting your business or just starting to write for your business you can introduce yourself in your first communication. Tell about your company, what you do, how it can help visitors, and explain your product or service line. You can do this in a sales letter or email, blog post, article, or newsletter. First communications are good places to give away a free introductory offer for your products or services.

Industry Information

Take a blogging or newsletter opportunity to educate readers about your industry. But be sure to make it fun or engaging. Try the prompt, "5 Things You Never Knew About..." Or develop a quiz about your industry with amusing scoring categories. These kinds of communications grab readers' attention. Think of how many Facebook quizzes you see in a given week. Or how many magazines offer quizzes to see what type of something or other you are.

These communication devices serve the dual purpose of throwing out a challenge that grabs readers' attention while educating them about your industry, and specifically about your business.

Guest Posts

Use friends and colleagues, in your industry and in related ones, to write guest posts for your blog. Credit the author for the post in the byline, and link it to his or her website. This tactic gives you fodder for your content machine. It comes from you although it is by someone else.

Get more from this method by having the author share the post throughout his or her social media. When you share, too, you both will have doubled your reaches.

Use Anecdotes

Relate an observation or incident from your daily life to your product or service, as discussed in Chapter 3. Stories about every day life make both you and your company relatable to potential clients. Many of my food posts told stories about my Nana's home cooking, or my dad's barbecues. I used this technique because my walks down memory lane got lots of comments, shares, and clicks. When you become just another pal to readers they want to share stories about themselves with you. They come to think of you as a friend, and as I've said before, it's hard to tell a friend you won't buy from her or him.

Jimmy Fallon and Ellen DeGeneres don't ask the most compelling questions of their guests, but viewers feel like they can goof around with them. Like when Ellen prank called people with the surname "Pilgrim" before Thanksgiving to ask them how to cook her turkey. Or when Jimmy Fallon used the "Looper" app on his iPad to record a doo-wop with Billy Joel right before our eyes. People relate to their harmless nonsense and let down their guards when they think of Ellen and Jimmy. You can do the same by making yourself relatable with a slice of your life now and then.

Use a TARDIS

"Dr. Who" fans will recognize this reference to time travel. For those who aren't familiar with that TV show a TARDIS (Time and Relative Dimension in Space) can transport riders to any time and any place in the universe. Take your readers back in time by telling a few historical facts about your industry or your business. Did you start out of a basement or spare bedroom? Are you located in a historic building or section of town? The Shinola Watch Company in Detroit uses their location in a landmark building to great effect in their marketing literature with the tagline, "Where America is Made."

I got a lot of mileage from my article about how attending a Paul McCartney concert took me through all the stages of my life. And my post on the history of sliced bread for National Sliced Bread Day got a response as if it were the greatest thing since . . . well, you know.

People love an occasional blast from the past and they enjoy speculation about the future, too. Think about where your product will be, or more importantly where customers who use your product will be, in 10, 15, 25, or even 50 years. Then write about it.

Be Dear Abby For a Day

Most of us receive questions or feedback from clients. If you aren't receiving any you should make sure your website comment and contact functions are working. Use the inquiries you get to write a question-and-answer column for your blog or newsletter. Don't be afraid to cite problems that were pointed out so you can brag about how you fixed them. Not only will it answer questions that other readers have, it will show you to be responsive to your client base.

And be sure to encourage comments. They can become a rich source of future Q&A columns, and even be used as testimonials, with the author's permission.

Use Holidays to Your Advantage

Every month has holidays. Some are federal or state ones, some religious, and most just silly. But they exist and serve as great writing prompts. For example one January, which is National Tea Month, I wrote a series called, "The 10 Days of Tea," to promote my touchscreen cookbooks. The series of 11 posts consisted of a set-up article to explain the series and then 10 more. Each of the succeeding posts discussed an unusual use of tea.

Readers received useful information and many had their interest peaked enough to buy my books. A hyperlocal news source picked up the series and syndicated it nationally. Every day, for 11 straight days, my post reigned supreme on front pages around the country.

Sticking with more traditional holidays, such as Independence Day, Labor Day, Thanksgiving, etc. is fine too. Mix up your writing and stand out from the crowd by connecting what you do to a holiday.

Be Like Snopes

Are you familiar with Snopes? It's a rumor-busting site that posts current, old, and recurring rumors usually found cycling around social media. The site features the rumor and then provides information to prove it either true or false.

Every industry and niche has its share of rumors. Write an article that discusses a common one about your industry, and either support it or bust it.

Give So You Will Receive

Readers always appreciate how-to tips. As discussed in Chapter 3, find a bit of knowledge you can pass along to readers to help them with something related to what you do. Don't solve all of their problems, but make sure what you give is useful, and causes readers to put you in the expert category with regard to your field.

Articles and blog posts containing how-tos can be converted into short Vine or You Tube videos, Power Points, and other slide shows to help you spread the word.

Many consultants in the financial, legal, and IT worlds deal with complex and cumbersome information. New products, or laws that affect existing tools or practices can blind side the average person. If you're in any of those fields, inform your client base of the changes and use clear, simple information to break it down for them. Explain what it means to them, and any financial or legal implications it can have. Then tell them what steps they need to take to avoid penalties, and be sure to tell them how you can help.

Buddy Up

When you buy a house you usually need professionals to help. Even with online services like Zillow and Realtor.com, most people still use realtors to list and show houses. When an offer to purchase is accepted buyers who are financing a portion of the purchase must obtain a loan. For that they need a mortgage banker or broker. If they've received good advice from their realtor, they will usually also want to use a home inspector. Moving services and storage facilities are also helpful resources.

Sellers benefit from using painters, cleaning services, carpet and flooring services, and handymen or contractors to get their homes ready to show. Professional staging services and even home managers, for vacant homes, are sometimes necessary. Most realtors have a group of sources that can perform all of these tasks, and more, for their clients. They form mini cartels, so to speak.

But they don't always maximize their relationships by marketing together. Who is in your professional wheelhouse? Your referral buddies can also serve as guest bloggers and collaborators on articles and posts. When two or more of you partner up to write an article, post, or newsletter, and all parties share it through social media, your reach is expanded exponentially.

Train for a Marathon, Not a Sprint

Giving away information that helps your customer or client pool to postpone buying from you now seems counterintuitive. But helping people to buy at just the right time for them can build trust and lasting relationships, too. Car sales people can remind their clients to change their oil, and can even partner with a local oil change shop to offer specials, or simply alert clients to when specials will happen.

Home designers and decorators can help clients move furnishings and accent pieces around their homes for a fresh look. Many will do this for a modest fee because they know that when their clients tire of the pieces, even in their new spots, they will be called on for redesigns and purchases.

My handyman has made a lot of money from me over the years because he fixes lots of things so I don't have to buy new ones. He also teaches me how to keep things running smoothly and how to do some things myself that I would otherwise have to pay him to do. Why would he walk away from a fee? Because he knows that I trust him to tell me when I need to pay him to do something. He knows that everything has a lifecycle and that when something reaches its end I will choose him to replace it. And he knows that I will refer him to my neighbors, friends, and relatives. He is training for the marathon and not the sprint.

Nothing leaves a worse taste in a person's mouth than feeling cheated. How do you feel when you realize that you bought something long before you needed to, and could have used that money for something else? Consider using the marathon strategy to building customer loyalty.

Say Thank You

Remember to thank your clients now and then. We all like to feel appreciated. Thanksgiving is an obvious time to do this. But when you get creative and find other times to show appreciation you can stand out from the crowd.

Consider April 1st or April Fools Day. When most people are looking for, or looking out for, "gotchas" turn that event on its head by showing your clients why they aren't fools for using you. Thank them with a token, a tip, or a special promotion. Make it as corny as "I'm not fooling, this special price is yours today," or relate it to something more connected to current events or pop culture. Or pick another event or holiday all together. Make it yours and become known for it.

New Releases

Most of us don't have new products or new pricing to release each week or month when we're communicating with our customer base via blog post or newsletter. But when you do have it use it. Tell readers all about it, how it can improve their businesses, make them more money, or make their lives easier.

Write often, and make sure whatever you write gives value.

Chapter 6

How to Make Your Writing SEO Friendly

Do you keep hearing about SEO but struggle to understand what it means? Or how to do it? SEO stands for search engine optimization. It means making any content that you put out into the wilds of the Internet easy for the search engines to find. Making content search-engine friendly helps it rise to the top of the results page when people search for what you do.

Most people click on the top two or three results on page one after searching for something. Few people go to the second or third results page. That means you have to prepare your content to get onto the first results page and the nearest to the top of that page as you can catapult it to generate clicks. You do this in a few ways.

But before you read about it, beware: search engines, especially Google, often change their formulas when too many users game the system. As an example it was possible a few years back to flood the Internet with links to your site. By getting my articles syndicated on a hyperlocal news source with outlets across the country I could put 900 links to my site out in a single article two or three times per week. Within one month my site was number three after the paid results section of the Google page. But Google caught on and changed its search method to look for quality, rather than quantity. So those who use my "here, there, and everywhere" strategy will now be penalized for it.

The best bet for the long haul is to feed the search engines, via your website and blog, with fresh, quality, content on a regular basis. But before you produce content you need keywords.

Keywords

Sometimes the simplest concepts can overwhelm us by seeming to be more complex than they are. If keywords make you feel that way, join the club. Then take a deep breath and relax, because the concept is really simple. Here it is in a nutshell.

Keywords are words people have been shown to use in searches that yield results similar to your site. You should have 5 or 6 good keywords to use in your content to tell the search engines that your site is a good place to find information about those keywords.

How do you choose them?

The best place to start is by boiling down the essence of what you do—what you want to be known for—into a list of about 25-30 words, or groups of two or three words. Try to put yourself into the mind of the person searching. Think about what problems a person would experience to need your product or services. And think about who your perfect customer or client would be. Make sure to include those kinds of things on your list. Then test them out.

Throw those words and terms into the search engine and see what comes up. If you've already got a website you'll appreciate seeing if and where your site is listed in the results.

It's a good idea to use a keyword-planning tool, too. Google has a free one connected to its AdSense product. Feed your keywords and phrases into it to find information about how many searches have been made using those terms. It will also show you how much competition the terms have. That information tells you:

1. If enough searches are done to make the keyword viable;

2. If too many other people are already using it.

Make Your Content Keyword Rich

Once you have selected your keywords use them. Make sure the content on each page of your site contains a keyword right up front and in a couple more spots further down in the text.

Don't overdo it. Your content has to feel natural. If you simply string together a bunch of keywords, or use them in a way that doesn't make sense, you won't fool the search engines and you'll be penalized for trying to trick them.

Share the Wealth With Your Blog Posts

Your articles and blog posts should contain keywords too. It probably won't be possible to use a keyword in the title of every post you publish, but it's a good idea to use them there when you can. Try to work a keyword into the first sentence of your copy and into the meta description too. That's the little blurb you see under the title of a search engine result.

Add Links

Insert links into your copy. If you use a byline, link it to your site. Find between one and three places within the copy that you can link to a place on your site. Doing so serves two purposes:

1. It puts fresh links to your site out into the internet which makes the search engines recognize you;

2. It drives readers to your site because many will click the links and land there.

Share, Share, and Share

Share your content in as many social media places as possible. Tweet it, share it on your Facebook Page, in LinkedIn Groups, on Google +. If your products or services lend themselves to visual media, like food, home décor, fashion, or art to name a few, share your pics on Instagram and Pinterest.

Make it easy for others to share your pearls of wisdom by placing share buttons beneath each blog post and in other places on your site. People will share if they like your content and if you make it easy for them to do it.

Get Backlinks

Get other sites to link back to you. Have colleagues and friends in ancillary industries put links to your site on theirs. They can put your link in a designated referral spot. Or you can offer to write a blog post for them to place on their sites that contains one or more links back to your site. Make sure to write one that has value to their client base.

Backlinks show search engines that your site is relevant, and also drive visitors to your site through clicks from the hosting site.

When Familiarity Can Breed Contempt

Like the fox in Aesop's fable whose frequent contact with the lion took the awe out of his sightings, search engines don't like to see the same article appearing all over the Internet. They want to see new content to consider your site awesome and move it up in their rankings.

An easy way to make this happen is to tweak your articles and posts for each place you publish them. Give each a new headline and alter about

30% of the content before you republish it so search engines think it is new and different. Then they will remain in awe of your site.

The moral of this story is to be consistent. Use your keywords in everything that you publish, and publish often and on a consistent schedule.

Chapter 7

You Don't Have to Be Matisse You Just Have to Paint

I love Bob Dylan's song "When I Paint My Masterpiece." In it he sings about all the wonderful ways in which his life will fall into place when he finally paints his masterpiece. I always took his point to be that you don't have to paint a masterpiece. You just have to seize the opportunities that each moment presents.

It's good to have dreams and big goals. But it's also good to realize that you reach them taking small steps, one at a time. Writing to reach clients is no different. Don't worry about reaching a million readers or going viral. Aim for 10, and then 50, and then 100. As your readership picks up steam sharing will help grow your reach exponentially.

None of this can happen until you make the first keystrokes. And unless you're a prodigy your first works aren't likely to go viral or to be masterpieces. That's okay. They don't need to be. They just need to be grammatically correct and give something of value.

Get The Party Started

Start by identifying a good point to make. You can take one from your stream of consciousness writings described in Chapter 3. Have something of value to give. Make sure the two are related to one another. For example, I used the annual Oscars Award Show to give communication tips. In that article I gave examples of how the show's host and presenters had succeeded or failed to do what I advised and showed the results of their communications as supporting evidence.

Set a word-count goal, or limit if you tend to be wordy. Then start to write and don't stop until you reach your word count goal. Just pour it all out. Don't stop to edit. Let it flow.

Let It Be

After you've written your piece, set it aside and let it rest. As Paul McCartney said, "Whisper words of wisdom," and then "let it be." Read it over again later in the day, and then again the next morning. In this way you let the ideas marinate and then gel.

Fix You

Like Cold Play, fix you(r) writing up. Do your first edit after you've let it rest awhile on the day you compose it. Sleep on it and take a fresh eye to your work. Then do another, finer edit. Clean up grammar, spelling and usage errors. Fine-tune your words. Cut out unnecessary language. Change things that don't make as much sense as they did when they poured off of your fingertips.

Let It Go

Once you've read and edited your work a couple of times, read it aloud to yourself. If you like the way it sounds and the flow is consistent, load it up to your site and let it go.

You've now started to feed the Internet beast with your keywords and links.

La Vie En Rose

Ernest Hemingway is considered a master writer of the 20th century. Gertrude Stein, known for her Parisian literary salon, had an influence on Hemingway's work early in his career. One of her most famous quotes is "A rose, is a rose, is a rose." She meant that repetition gets your point across. Whether or not you like Hemingway or Stein her formula worked and helped to establish "Hem" as one of the greatest writers of his time.

Feed the beast often. Give it good food. It will grow.

Chapter 8

Pull from Popular Culture

One of the best ways to make your writing relatable is to connect it to something in popular culture. Unless you're writing for posterity, your work does not need to stand the test of time. It simply needs to grab readers' attention and hold it long enough to peak their interest in you.

So much content flows through the Internet each day it won't matter if yours is dated in two or three years. Especially when you keep feeding the beast with fresh meat.

Borrowing from popular culture is an easy way to stay current. Just be careful to select the right events and media. Your audience needs to be aware of your reference for it to resonate with them. That takes you back to the beginning. Who is your audience? Who will be most likely to buy your product or service? Who is it designed to help? Consider these things when choosing what to reference in your writing.

If your potential customer base is more than 40 years of age, Moon Taxi or snap chatting will probably not make meaningful references.

Most everyone is aware of big events like The Super Bowl, The World Series, The Academy Awards, and The Grammys. Individual movies, books, and music are more niche-oriented. It's important to know if your niche is likely to be familiar with those things before referring to them.

Fads come and go, but so does web content. Mood rings and pet rocks were big in the 1970's; Rubik's cubes in the '80's; beanie babies and boys bands in the '90's; Crocs and iPods in the aught decade; dog shaming and twerking in the 20-teens. Have some fun referencing fads to help you make a point that adds value to your audience.

Watch your parlance, though. If you are a hipster, and you sell to hipsters, go ahead and write like one. If you aren't one, but most people will have heard a catch phrase you want to use in a headline or opening sentence, use it, and reference its origin. Be sure that enough of the people you're trying to reach will know what you are referring to.

Industry specific language often sails over the heads of potential clients. You may be knowledgeable about why the technical aspects of a product or service make it perfect for your client base. But unless they are as technically competent as you are, you need to translate your techno-talk into plain English and use some examples they can relate to.

I love my Apple products. But I don't know the technical reasons why their features do what they do. And I don't want to. I just want to know what the features can do for me and how to use them.

If you're not marketing to people within your niche of your own industry, find examples that mean something to them to get them excited about your brand.

That takes us back to popular culture because it's everywhere. You didn't have to read or see The Hunger Games or Gone Girl to know of their existence and the gist of their storylines. And simply knowing who played in the Super Bowl and who starred in its commercials will usually be enough for you to catch the drift of statements about it. Making reference to a big popular culture phenomenon will work with the majority of the people the majority of the time.

Chapter 9

Keep to the Middle of the Road

The less controversial you are, the more business readers you will attract and keep.

Be Politically Astute

Are you from a red state or a blue one?

Do you consider yourself a Democrat or a Republican? Or, if you're into rebranding, are you a Progressive or a Conservative? Or a Libertarian?

In the age of political correctness you'll appeal to the most people by staying apolitical. Unless you are selling a product, service, or idea for a political organization you will almost certainly alienate at least half of the reading public by taking a political position. We all have them. But in the workplace it's best to check them at the door.

Several polls show the top five political issues in America as having close percentages for and against them. The majority shown depends upon the pollster releasing the data, but they are all near the middle. That means that we each have nearly a 50% chance of alienating anyone we choose to discuss a political issue with. So unless you're a political operative, writer, or commentator you'll probably grow your business and your career trajectory best by keeping your leanings to yourself.

This advice applies to all written materials and communications you have with clients or potential clients.

See the Light About Religion

Religion is and has always been an intensely personal matter. Our religious beliefs are kept close to our hearts. People have died for religion throughout history. Because it evokes intense emotions it's easy to inadvertently offend readers when making religious references in business writing.

There are many religions, big and small. And while religion is a big part of American culture, it's not a part of culture that is likely to forward your branding efforts and grow your client base unless the religion you wish to write about happens to be the niche you market to. For most of us, that won't be the case.

So it's better kept in the "hands off" category when creating content to market or brand your business. Stick to popular culture to find reference points to reach the average person.

Chapter 10

Stay the Course

The best way to stay on readers' radar is to make it easy for them to find you. Once they've made an initial connection due to your use of good SEO practices and networking, readers will continue to tune in if they know when and where you broadcast.

Did you know that "Seinfeld," "Everybody Loves Raymond," and "The Office" were almost cancelled before they made it big? All three shows benefited from moving to time slots where the right people tuned in. And once viewers found the shows, they stayed dedicated to them.

High Frequency

People who write and publish everyday grow the largest audiences and do it in the shortest period. But people who do that are generally writers paid for daily content production. Publishing three times per week is considered ideal for growing a blog following. Remember my Chapter 1 examples of frequent communications. Quantity usually trumps quality. But even if you can only publish once per week you will still be ahead of much of your competition.

Whichever frequency you are able to keep up announce to your readership when and where they can find your publications. And then make sure you show up. Most times it will be on your website or blog. But some business people also publish their musings on other open source sites such as Patch.com, Forbes.com, and OpenSalon. com. Wherever you publish set a regular schedule and stick to it so readers can find you.

If you tend to forget to write, schedule your writing sessions and publishing times on your calendar.

Length

Attention spans being what they are today, less is often more in writing. This is especially true in blogs. People scroll through email and websites and click on titles or pictures that look interesting. They won't linger for long, so you've got to get their attention fast. Do it by pulling them right in with a surprising fact for an opening statement or a question. And then keep it moving. Make your sentences short and to the point so readers don't get tangled up in complex language or sentence construction. Once you've hooked them make your point and get out.

Spoon-feeding readers with short bursts of information has two benefits:

1. It holds readers interest.

2. It gives you more topics to write about in subsequent publications.

The best-read blog posts don't exceed 400 words. If you can't make your full point in that amount of words consider breaking your post down into two or three parts to publish as three separate posts.

Articles can be a little longer, with the best ones weighing in between 700-1000 words.

Headlines

Use of clever headlines is the best way to grab readers' attention. They should not exceed five words. Don't let your cleverness conceal what your point is, though. Make sure your headline is related to your article.

Openers

Try to use one of your keywords right up front in the first sentence. And then engage the reader immediately. Sometimes asking a question is the easiest way to do that. Good opening questions include:

"Have you ever . . . ?"
"How many times . . . ?"
"Do you remember . . . ?"
"Did you know . . . ?"

Whenever possible make your writing entertaining. And remember to use examples that your target audience can relate to.

Above all, have fun with your writing. Incorporate your own observations and slices of your life into the points you make to your readers. Let them get to know you and find ways to get to know them. Make them loyal to you with the value your writings add to their businesses and their lives. And enjoy watching your business grow!